THE HUMAN BEHIND THE HERO

JASON MOMOA IS AQUAMAN®

HOT TOPICS

KRISTEN RAJCZAK NELSON

Gareth Stevens PUBLISHING

Please visit our website, www.garethstevens.com. For a free color catalog of all our high-quality books, call toll free 1-800-542-2595 or fax 1-877-542-2596.

Library of Congress Cataloging-in-Publication Data
Names: Rajczak Nelson, Kristen, author.
Title: Jason Momoa is Aquaman / Kristen Rajczak Nelson.
Description: Buffalo, New York : Gareth Stevens Publishing, [2023] | Series: The human behind the hero | Includes bibliographical references and index.
Identifiers: LCCN 2022019959 (print) | LCCN 2022019960 (ebook) | ISBN 9781538283837 (paperback) | ISBN 9781538283851 (library binding) | ISBN 9781538283868 (ebook)
Subjects: LCSH: Momoa, Jason–Juvenile literature. | Motion picture actors and actresses–United States–Biography–Juvenile literature. | Aquaman (Motion picture)–Juvenile literature. | Aquaman (Fictitious character)–Juvenile literature.
Classification: LCC PN2287.M658 R35 2023 (print) | LCC PN2287.M658 (ebook) | DDC 791.4302/8092 [B]–dc23/eng/20220524
LC record available at https://lccn.loc.gov/2022019959
LC ebook record available at https://lccn.loc.gov/2022019960

First Edition

Published in 2023 by
Gareth Stevens Publishing
2544 Clinton St
Buffalo, NY 14224

Designer: Rachel Rising
Editor: Kristen Rajczak Nelson

Photo credits: Cover, p. 1 Image Press Agency / Alamy Stock Photo; Cover, pp.1-32 KID_A/Shutterstock.com; Cover, pp. 1-32 gn8/Shutterstock.com; pp. 5, 25 DFree/Shutterstock.com; p. 7 CarlaVanWagoner/Shutterstock.com; p. 9 https://commons.wikimedia.org/wiki/File:Diamond_Head_Hawaii_-_panoramio.jpg; p. 11 s_bukley/Shutterstock.com; pp. 13, 21, 29 Kathy Hutchins/Shutterstock.com; p. 15 Tinseltown/Shutterstock.com; p. 17 ZUMA Press, Inc. / Alamy Stock Photo; p. 19 Jaguar PS/Shutterstock.com; pp. 23,27 Cubankite/Shutterstock.com.

Printed in the United States of America

CPSIA compliance information: Batch #CW23GS: For further information contact Gareth Stevens at 1-800-542-2595.

CONTENTS

BORN AND RAISED

Jason Momoa was born on August 1, 1979, in Honolulu, Hawaii. His dad was Hawaiian. But Jason moved to Iowa with his mom when he was young. Around age 12, Jason started spending his summers in Hawaii with his dad.

BEHIND THE SCENES

JASON SPENT A LOT OF TIME IN THE WATER WHEN HE WAS IN HAWAII. HE LOVES THE OCEAN.

Jason liked where he grew up in Iowa. But there wasn't much **diversity** there. He didn't look like other kids he knew. Sometimes he felt like he was from two different worlds: Hawaii and Iowa.

BEHIND THE SCENES

IN ADDITION TO BEING HAWAIIAN, JASON IS PART GERMAN, IRISH, AND NATIVE AMERICAN.

GETTING STARTED

Jason wanted to go to school in Hawaii. His dad encouraged him to stay on the mainland to learn all he could. Jason studied **marine biology** in college. He later left school, though, and moved to Hawaii. That's where his **career** began!

BEHIND THE SCENES

THE MORE TIME JASON SPENT IN HAWAII, THE MORE HE FELT CONNECTED TO ITS CULTURE, OR THE WAY PEOPLE LIVED THERE, AND HIS HAWAIIAN FAMILY MEMBERS.

At 19, Jason got his first acting job. At the **audition**, Jason said he was a successful model. He wasn't a model and had no other **experience**. Still, he got the job on *Baywatch: Hawaii,* which aired from 1999 to 2001.

BEHIND THE SCENES

FOR YEARS, ARTICLES ABOUT JASON SAID HE WAS A MODEL, ALL BASED ON A LIE HE SAYS HE TOLD AT HIS FIRST AUDITION!

TV WORK

Jason followed *Baywatch* with two more TV shows. He had a leading role, or part, on a show called *North Shore.* He appeared on *Stargate: Atlantis* from 2005 to 2009. He started to get more attention.

BEHIND THE SCENES

JASON LOVES TO PLAY GUITAR AND BASS, AMONG OTHER INSTRUMENTS. HE BRINGS THEM TO THE SETS WHERE HE WORKS!

Not long after, Jason auditioned for a new **fantasy** show. The character didn't have much **dialogue**. So, instead of speaking at first, Jason did a dance called the haka. That helped him get the part of Khal Drogo on *Game of Thrones*.

BEHIND THE SCENES

THE HAKA COMES FROM THE MAORI, A GROUP NATIVE TO NEW ZEALAND. IT'S OFTEN PRACTICED IN HAWAII IN MANY FORMS. PEOPLE YELL AND STICK THEIR TONGUES OUT TO SCARE THE ENEMY!

THE BIG MAN

Games of Thrones started in 2011. Khal Drogo didn't say much, but he had a popular story on the show and a fearsome look. That same year, Jason towered on the big screen as Conan in *Conan the Barbarian.*

BEHIND THE SCENES

JASON IS HARD TO MISS! HE'S AROUND 6 FEET, 4 INCHES (1.9 M) TALL!

INTO THE WATER

In 2014, news came out that Jason was going to play the superhero Aquaman! Like Jason, Aquaman is from two different worlds. Aquaman is from the underwater kingdom of Atlantis and lived on Earth as Arthur Curry.

BEHIND THE SCENES

IN THE ORIGINAL AQUAMAN COMICS, AQUAMAN IS WHITE AND HAS BLOND HAIR. JASON WAS PROUD TO BRING SOME DIVERSITY TO THE PART.

Jason first appeared as Aquaman in 2016. He was in a short scene in *Batman v Superman: Dawn of Justice*. Then he became one of the stars of *Justice League* in 2017. Jason's Aquaman was one of the most fun parts of the movie!

BEHIND THE SCENES

AQUAMAN IS SUPERSTRONG, CAN BREATHE UNDERWATER, AND CAN TALK TO CREATURES UNDER THE SEA, SUCH AS FISH.

SUPER WORK

It takes a lot of work to look like a superhero—and Jason doesn't like gym workouts! But he does like rock climbing. When filming *Aquaman*, he had his own rock-climbing wall on set! He also did a lot of training with swords to fight like Aquaman.

BEHIND THE SCENES

AQUAMAN IS OFTEN SHOWN WITH A TRIDENT, OR A SPEAR WITH THREE POINTS.

Aquaman came out in December 2018. It made more than $1 billion around the world! Jason cared most about two people who saw the movie: his children. He was so happy to star in a movie he could take them to see!

BEHIND THE SCENES

JASON HAS TWO CHILDREN, NAKOA-WOLF AND LOLA. HE BROUGHT THEM TO VISIT THE SET OF *JUSTICE LEAGUE*!

Jason started filming *Aquaman and the Lost Kingdom* in 2021. He said it was hard work and he got hurt a lot! That year, Jason showed off his sword skills some more as Duncan Idaho in the movie *Dune*.

BEHIND THE SCENES

IN MARCH 2021, A DIFFERENT **VERSION** OF *JUSTICE LEAGUE* CAME OUT. IT GAVE FANS EVEN MORE TIME WITH JASON AS AQUAMAN!

DIVING INTO THE FUTURE

Aquaman and the Lost Kingdom came out in 2023. And Jason may not be done carrying the trident yet! Jason has become a star as the superhero Aquaman. What else will he do?

BEHIND THE SCENES

JASON HAS HIS OWN PRODUCTION COMPANY, OR A COMPANY THAT WANTS TO MAKE MOVIES. IT'S CALLED PRIDE OF GYPSIES.

TIMELINE

1979 JASON MOMOA IS BORN ON AUGUST 1 IN HAWAII.

1999 HE IS ON TV FOR THE FIRST TIME IN *BAYWATCH: HAWAII.*

2005 JASON BEGINS APPEARING ON *STARGATE: ATLANTIS.*

2011 HE STARS IN *CONAN THE BARBARIAN*. HE APPEARS *ON GAME OF THRONES.*

2016 JASON APPEARS AS AQUAMAN FOR THE FIRST TIME IN *BATMAN V SUPERMAN: DAWN OF JUSTICE.*

2017 HE APPEARS IN *JUSTICE LEAGUE.*

2018 JASON STARS IN *AQUAMAN*. IT GOES ON TO MAKE $1 BILLION WORLDWIDE!

2021 HE APPEARS IN *DUNE* AND *ZACK SNYDER'S JUSTICE LEAGUE.*

2023 *AQUAMAN AND THE LOST KINGDOM* COMES OUT.

FOR MORE INFORMATION

BOOKS

DeConnick, Kelly Sue, et al. *Aquaman: Volume 1, Unspoken Water.* Burbank, CA: DC Comics, 2019.

London, Martha. *Jason Momoa.* Lake Elmo, MN: Focus Readers, 2021.

WEBSITES

Aquaman | DC
www.dccomics.com/characters/aquaman
Find out more about the character Aquaman from DC Comics here.

Warner Bro.com | Aquaman Movie
www.warnerbros.com/movies/aquaman
Check out behind-the-scenes of Aquaman and find out how to watch it.

Publisher's note to educators and parents: Our editors have carefully reviewed these websites to ensure that they are suitable for students. Many websites change frequently, however, and we cannot guarantee that a site's future contents will continue to meet our high standards of quality and educational value. Be advised that students should be closely supervised whenever they access the internet.

GLOSSARY

audition: A try out.

career: The job someone chooses to do for a long time.

dialogue: The things a character says in a book or movie.

diversity: The state of having different races or cultures of people in a community.

experience: Skills earned by doing something.

fantasy: Having to do with a story that takes place in an imaginary world.

marine biology: The study of life in the ocean.

version: A form of something that is different from others.

INDEX